Scottish Birds

by A. B. Lees

JAMES PIKE LTD
St Ives, Cornwall, England

The author and publishers wish to thank Mr. Robin Lees for the use of his photographs on bottom page 18, bottom page 20 and page 25; line drawings were produced by Mr. T. Beer.

First Edition 1975

ISBN 0 85932 095 2

Printed by: H S (Litho) Ltd
Weston-Super-Mare, Somerset

Introduction

Scotland is inexhaustible in its supply of holidays for the ornithologist and, as one looks back, it is quite impossible to decide upon a favourite. All are crammed with perfect moments - idyllic or exciting. This does sound horribly sentimental but it is quite simply true. Few other holiday areas inspire such affection and loyalty, or such feelings of anticipation and delight upon return after a year or more spent elsewhere.

There is good birding to be had every season of the year. Birds will vary according to the time of year. The auks (puffins, guillemots, and razorbills) should be at their ledges in April, though they may be late if the weather is bad. They leave during August, so make it July to be safe. Fulmars and gannets stay rather longer. Rarities are more likely on passage in spring and autumn which are good times for waders. The vast flocks of geese and duck can be seen in winter.

Spring is perhaps the best time. There will still be some geese about and you'll see those superb skeins over the hills as they head for their breeding grounds in the far north. The seabirds will be arriving. Eagles, greenshank, capers, and indeed everything else, will be displaying, while the blackcock will be at their leks. Midges will not have driven the deer to the high tops. From mid-August to mid-October deer stalking makes access difficult in the hills. Grouse moors too will be affected from August 12th. May and June are good months also as young birds are being fed then. A one inch ordnance survey map of your area is invaluable and adds greatly to the interest of expeditions.

Southern Scotland

The Border National Forest Park is the largest planted forest in Britain and it is possible to enter the Kielder Forest in Northumberland and drive along the good forest roads and come out in Scotland. Long-eared owl, woodcock and black grouse breed, as well as other species. Once in Southern Scotland the best known bird areas seem to be either to the east or the west. To the east near Coldstream is the Hirsel, seat of the Earls of Home, and an excellent place for birds both in summer and winter. Pièd flycatchers nest, and woodpeckers, woodcock, tawny

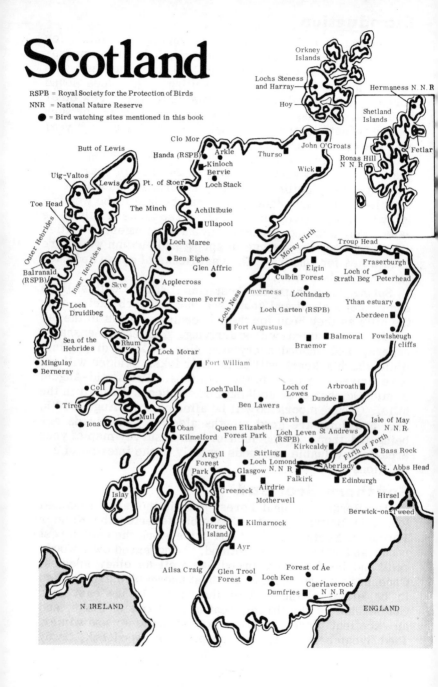

owl, lesser redpoll and redstart are among the 96 recorded breeding species. There are many other well watered valleys in the Tweed, Teviot, Jed Water and Eden River areas, where kingfisher, dippers, grey wagtails, goosanders and sandpipers enhance the quiet beauty. The dipper is a fascinating bird to watch as it bobs up and down on a rock in midstream or walks along the river bed under water to feed. It is easy to watch as it is very territorial and unwilling to leave its stretch of river. When it is followed to the limits of its territory it will double back again.

Just north of Greenlaw is Hule Moss which has a loch. Pinkfeet and duck are found there in autumn and to a lesser degree in winter and spring. Permission should be sought from the farmer at Hollyburton Farm three miles North West of Greenlaw on a minor road.

Out on the east coast at St. Abb's Head there are fine cliffs with breeding seabirds. Near North Berwick too the air around the Bass Rock is thick with seabirds and clamorous with their cries. The Bass Rock is famous for its large gannet colony - 6,000 to 8,000 pairs of Sula bassana-ital. Its other name is solan goose, though it is not a goose at all. It is thought that solan may come from the Gaelic sula (sulan eye) and indicate sharpness of sight. The gannet has large eyes and must have exceptional sight, for it dives from up to 100 feet into the sea to catch fish. Gannets fishing in a bay provide hours of fascinated watching. Contact the boatmen at North Berwick for access to the Bass Rock. A trip round it is a great experience. Gannets are in residence from May to September. Fulmars can be seen on the walls of Tantallon Castle. The spread of the fulmar in this century has been most interesting. Until 1878 it bred only on St. Kilda but there are now colonies almost all round the British coasts.

Near Edinburgh is Aberlady Bay, a very popular nature reserve. It is important to get there at the turn of the tide. This is so with most estuaries - they are at their best for an hour or so after high tide. The receding tide exposes the birds' food but at low tide all you see are endless mudflats. Go east from Aberlady to the car park by a small bridge over the Peffer Burn. You can walk over the saltings to Gullane Point. This is an excellent place at all times of the year, and especially for rarities on passage in spring and autumn. It is the best place in Scotland for wood sandpipers and at Gullane Point red-necked grebes may be seen. The list of waders and duck is extensive. Gosford Bay to the west is also a good spot. At Seafield, east of Leith docks, sewage outfall attracts thousands of duck, especially scaup, in winter.

Duddingston Loch is a nature reserve, only $1\frac{1}{2}$ miles from the centre of Edinburgh. Access is not allowed, but many of the roads in Holyrood Park offer good views and at Duddingston Foreshore the loch meets the park. Duck can be seen in winter and the two commoner grebes, tufted duck, pochard and long-eared owl breed.

South west Scotland has some first rate habitats in beautiful surroundings. The best known is the Caerlaverock National Nature Reserve. The whole area from above Glancapel round to the estuary of the Lochar is excellent and has a wide fringe of salt marsh known as the Merse. Above Glencapel is a good place for whooper swans and the road for some miles there commands fine views of the wildfowl, (geese, duck and waders) that collect in great numbers in winter. Barnacle geese may exceed 3,000 while up to 10,000 pinkfeet winter in the Solway Firth. There are smaller numbers of greylag. The distribution of barnacles in Britain is interesting. Ringing has revealed that the Solway flocks come from Spitzbergen, while the barnacles of Islay and the Scottish islands breed in Greenland. The barnacles that breed in Siberia spend the winter in Holland and Germany. All three groups are quite distinct.

The west side of the Nith estuary is equally attractive and the backcloth of Criffell rising to nearly 2,000 feet lends it added charm. You can view Carse Sands from the A710 or get down to the sea at Carsethorn and Southerness Point. Duck and waders are the chief attraction: wigeon, pintail, scaup, scoter, knot, redshank, or indeed almost any wader. Keep a look out here and on the Caerlaverock side for geese feeding in the fields. On the rocks at Southerness Point there may be purple sandpiper and large flocks of knot. Until the beginning of this century the exact breeding ground of the knot and the sanderling was unknown because they breed so far north on the high Arctic tundra. The sanderling differs from other waders in having no hind toe though this is difficult to distinguish as it scampers along at the very edge of the waves.

Carlingwark Loch just south of Castle Douglas can be

seen from the A75, and then the minor road going north from Bridge of Dee is worthwhile and will bring you to Loch Ken. A minor road goes up the west side for several miles and the A762 runs along the shore for 4 miles at the northern end. These areas are all good for geese, including bean geese and Greenland white-fronts, and for duck, such as wigeon, goldeneye, pintail and goosander.

North West of Loch Ken lies the Glentrool National Forest Park. It can be entered by turning right at Bargrennan off the A714 from Newton Stewart. Many birds breed,

Pied Flycatcher

including ring ouzel, black grouse, dipper, pied flycatcher, woodcock and redstart. The Rhinns of Kells are included in this area. They are wild and isolated and may hold eagle and peregrine and certainly golden plover. A smaller forest to the east in a most beautiful area is the Forest of Ae. The minor road off the A76 at Closeburn, 3 miles south of Thornhill, goes through beautiful country past a large rookery and climbs into the forest. Sparrow hawks breed here. Kinnel Water, further east still, is attractive country and so is the area all round Thornhill.

Down in the South West corner of Wigtown, Mochrum Loch has a unusual freshwater colony of cormorants. The muddy area at the head of Loch Ryan is good for grey lag geese, duck and waders. At the very southern tip of Scotland the cliffs of the Mull of Galloway have colonies of seabirds. Permission can be sought from the keepers to enter the lighthouse area. The upper part of Wigtown Bay north of Spittal has wide sands and saltings. The west side is the better for geese, duck and waders but it is not easy to get at.

Ailsa Craig lies off the coast of Ayr opposite Girvan.

Unless you can get on one of the few trips that go round the island, so that the tremendous seabird colonies can be viewed from the boat, you need to camp overnight. All this needs to be arranged in advance. Write to Publicity Dept. , Town Clerk's Office at Girvan. Around 13,000 pairs of gannets breed and many other seabirds can be seen there. Up in the hills behind Girven are attractive valleys where small inns can be found. Horse Island just off the coast at Ardrossan has five species of breeding gulls and three of terns. It belongs to the R.S.P.B. and free permits can be obtained from their honorary warden in Ardrossan. Inland to the North East the southern end of Castle Semple Loch is excellent in the winter for wildfowl.

East Coast and Moray Firth Area

The first stop for bird watchers, after crossing the Forth Bridge on the journey up the east coast, will not be on the coast at all, but at the National Nature Reserve of Loch Leven. It lies near the pleasant town of Kinross. Leave the M90 at junction 5 and make for the R.S.P.B. centre at Vane Farm on the B9097. They have an attractive room with much to interest youngsters - and their parents ! There are devices to test your bird recognition, and you can brush up your knowledge of bird song by listening to recordings. There's a telescope for viewing the loch. A nature trail goes up the hill behind the farm through woods with redstarts and lesser redpolls, and on to the moor for red grouse and curlew. Bird-wise the loch itself may be rather disappointing in summer, though tufted duck, gadwall and shoveler breed, but at all other seasons it holds geese, especially pinkfeet and greylag. It seems to be the assembly point for pinkfeet when they arrive in Scotland from Iceland and Greenland where they have bred. Later some of them disperse to other parts for the winter, but in autumn, from late September onwards, there may be 12,000 of them on Loch Leven. You should also see the wild whooper swans then, with their bright yellow and black bills and straight necks - so much more attractive than the orange-billed mute swan. Perhaps part of their magic lies in the knowledge that they may have come straight from nesting in Arctic Russia.

Drive slowly along the road to Vane Farm. There should be geese feeding in the fields between the road and the loch, often very close. In April we have watched curlew feeding on the plough-land just over the hedge, and could see them picking up and swallowing earthworms.

Out on the coast, 'golfing widows and orphans' can turn a visit to St. Andrews to good advantage. The Eden estuary is an excellent place for waders and duck. You will easily notice the shelduck; a large, showy, black and white duck with a red bill and a bright tan band round its fore part. In spring and autumn the handsome black-tailed godwit is fairly common. Walk out from the golf links to Shelly Point and Out Head. Another good area is around Guard Bridge. If you go on up the A919 and B945 towards Tayport you can turn off on the right to Morton Lochs. There are many breeding duck and waders in summer. Viewing is from the road, or there are hides needing permits from Nature Conservancy. Beyond the lochs is Tentsmuir reserve - no cars allowed. Long-tailed duck collect in numbers off the point in early spring. They are fascinating to watch; noisy and talkative and very active, often all diving at once. The drake has a lovely call.

Nine miles south of St. Andrews at Pittenweem you can get a boat to the Isle of May which lies 5 miles off shore. It is famous as a landfall for migrants and in September and May there is no knowing what rarity you may have the luck to light on. A lot depends on the wind - it's likely to be exciting after easterlies. In summer there are nesting sea birds and in autumn Manx and sooty shearwaters are often to be seen on the water.

The Firth of Tay is a good area for bird watching. In autumn and winter geese roost on the mud banks and there are also many duck and waders of all kinds. In the Newburgh area the goldeneye is frequently to be seen in spring. The drake has handsome black and white plumage with a white patch in front of its eye. The duck is beautiful too, with chocolate brown head and soft grey back. Little gulls are difficult to find in Britain, but one of the best places to try is the Buddon Burn about a mile east of Monifieth. Spring is the ideal time. Watch for them too along the coasts of Fife and Angus in summer and autumn.

Do make time, before going on up the coast, to visit the Loch of Lowes near Dunkeld. Take the A9 north out of the town, turn right on to the A923 and after about $1\frac{1}{2}$ miles a turning on the right will be sign-posted to the reserve.

Ospreys nest here. They have not received as much publicity as the Loch Garten birds, but the hide is much closer
to the nest and you may well have superb views of these
magnificently marked brown and white birds. They have
usually arrived by mid-April and you can view them from
the hide at once. After finding Loch Garten bolted and
barred for the 'settling in' period, we came straight down
to the Loch of Lowes and had wonderful views. And there's
a great deal more to be seen beside the ospreys - goosander,
teal, goldeneye, great crested grebe and they have had a
nesting pair of Slavonian grebe. Surely it must be at the
southern point of its range? Another impressive sight is
the vast flocks of geese which fly in to roost on the loch in
the evening. The sound of wings and voices is not soon forgotten. A twenty four hour watch is kept on the ospreys'
nest. It seems these birds are making a slow but most
welcome return to Scotland, where they died out at the
beginning of the century as a result of the depredations of
'naturalist's'. Hunters would be a better description.
Charles St. John's account of a tour in Sutherland in the
mid-nineteenth century makes incredible reading. After
describing how he shot the female osprey, took her eggs
and watched the male calling disconsolately, he ends 'I
was really sorry I had shot her'. But his penitence did
not last long! Three chapters later he is repeating the
performance.

Back on the coast, visitors to Carnoustie, Arbroath and
Montrose may see terns nesting on the less frequented
beaches and sea birds on the cliffs, especially between
Arbroath and Lunan Bay. Skuas turn up off shore in late
summer.

Don't neglect the inland areas of Angus. Around Forfar
there are three roadside lochs, Forfar, Balgavies and
Rescobie where you can watch from your car. Mute and
whooper swans are likely and lots of duck: goldeneye,
wigeon, shoveler, pochard and tufted. There are beautiful
glens too: Glen Esk, Glen Prosen and Glen Clova. Here
are all the birds of Scottish burn and glen - dippers, grey
wagtails with splashes of yellow as well as grey, redstarts
and long-tailed tits. Angus is indeed good birding country.

On up the coast to Fowlsheugh cliffs. This is a 'must'.
Heugh means crag or quarry, so it would seem that this
spot has been famous for its sea bird colonies from time

immemorial. Turn off the A92 about 3 miles south of Stonehaven for Crawton, and go on till the road ends at the sea. The one inch ordnance survey map is useful here. Crawton appears to be a couple of farms. Park your car, allowing for the passage of farm vehicles, and take the path north along the cliffs. This mile of conglomerate cliff is rather unusual in appearance but its formation is of great assistance to bird watchers. Its mini-indentations mean that you always have a crowded - over-crowded! - sea bird colony just opposite you. Perfect viewing of bird slums! Thousands of guillemots and razorbills occupy every inch of space; also kittiwakes, fulmars and puffins. Between April and the end of July is the time; and with sunshine on the sea and clumps of pink thrift it's a perfect spot.

But there's another to come. The phrase 'one of the best birdwatching areas' gets sadly overworked when describing Scotland. The Ythan estuary must surely deserve that title. As you leave Newburgh, 13 miles north of Aberdeen, the road runs beside the estuary for 2 miles. The estuary is narrow and viewing is close. In spring and summer there are hundreds of eiders. This is a large duck and perhaps the most beautiful one. The drake's breeding plumage of pink breast and lime green on its neck has a delicacy that cannot be imagined from pictures. It must be seen, and nowhere better than at the Ythan. The soft crooning call is an added attraction. In winter and early spring the estuary will produce pinkfeet and greylag and a great variety of duck, among them musical parties of long-tailed duck. Always there are masses of waders and in summer terns breed on the Sands of Forvie Nature Reserve. The entrance to the reserve is at Collieston, north of the estuary. Turn off on B9003. Permits necessary in the breeding season from the Scottish Nature Conservancy.

As you drive on to Cruden Bay keep a look out for geese feeding in the fields. All this North East corner of Scotland is rich farming land, full of sheep, cattle - and geese! Just beyond Cruden Bay are the Bullers of Buchan, granite cliffs this time, where kittiwakes and fulmars breed.

Nine miles north of Peterhead leave the A952 and turn right on to minor roads towards Old Rattray and Seatown. The Loch of Strathbeg is the creation of a great storm in 1715 and is fringed by extensive sand dunes. The south end of the loch may also be watched from the road near a derelict chapel. In summer eiders and great crested grebe will be nesting. Both are attractive birds to watch. In winter and spring there's a vast array of duck, geese, and swans, and of course migrant waders.

Just before you leave Aberdeenshire along its north coast on B9031 you must drop down the steep hill to the tiny hamlet of Pennan. There, enclosed by Pennan Head and the cliffs rising to more distant Troup Head, you will find a delightful bay - and the Pennan Inn. The proprietors have the pleasant habit of sending their guests of the past year a Christmas card. Not that you are likely to need reminding of your visit. Troup Head is unforgettable and the Pennan Inn is a good place to stay. You'll need rest and refreshment after the steep climb up to Pennan Head, where you walk along the cliffs with magnificent views, and a chance of seeing the peregrine which nests here. The slope of the grassy cliffs makes them dangerous, so this is a place for adults only. Troup Head really demands a day's expedition - you won't want to leave. A day spent in the sunshine on the old red sandstone cliffs will be a red-letter day indeed. The busy world is miles away, and there's only you, and the sea, and the cliffs, and the birds. The headland is extensive and each view seems perfect - till you see the next one. Puffins, guillemots, razorbills, fulmars and kittiwakes abound and there are house martins nesting in a cave at the eastern end. To reach the headland go towards Banff on B9031 but soon turn right for Northfield Farm where you may leave the car. It seems rather an imposition on the farmer, especially as there is no footpath, but when we asked permission we were very helpfully received. Let us hope that no bad manners on the part of bird watchers will mar future welcomes. Bottles, tins and plastic are disgusting litter, but they are also very dangerous to farm stock. You walk north to a gully and along its left side to the sea. Peregrines may be found here too.

Inland at Hatton Castle near Turiff, there's the largest rookery in the British Isles and probably in the world. It is in private ground but you can see rooks feeding in the fields everywhere. To a Sassenach, it often seems that the rook should be the emblem of Scotland, and up the east side they are particularly common. Scotland provides the large areas of open agricultural land that they like.

The Moray Firth is popular with ornithologists. Findhorn Bay, north of Forres, is an attractive place. The road is right beside the bay at the village of Findhorn, but there are various by-roads leading north from Forres to the south side of the bay. One must explore and find out where the birds are. Goosanders, mergansers, goldeneye, wigeon, teal, bar-tailed godwits, shelduck, oystercatchers, geese, and hundreds of redshank have all been seen in an hour's visit.

Shelduck

Between the bay and Nairn, stretches 6 miles of the Culbin Forest. Exciting species nest here: crested tit, capercaillie, siskin, woodcock crossbill, long-tailed tit, goldcrest and treecreeper. Terns nest on the long sand bar off shore, and the saltings between the bar and the forest are excellent for duck and waders. It's a good walk through the forest to the sea, but at certain times permission to take a car may be obtained from the head forester at Kintessack. This is more likely if you can avoid the weekends. Contact him on arrival, and if you are an early riser you may get permission to go in at dawn, when you are very likely to have fine views of capers. In early morning these big turkey like birds come out on to the rides. The cocks display, uttering a strange call that has been likened to the popping of corks! Look for them, as well, on the big water tanks in Culbin. Smoking is absolutely prohibited in the forest and its edges, and if you have your car park it on hard ground without vegetation.

The inner Moray Firth area is full of bird life at all seasons. Both east and west of Inverness the road goes along the seashore and also near Fortrose and on the

B9039 towards Fort George. Udale Bay on Cromarty Firth is excellent. At all these places you can watch from your car. Chanonry Point is good too, and near Redcastle hundreds of goosanders and mergansers may be seen in autumn. There is a heronry at Munlochy and fulmars nest on the cliffs at the Sutors and Rosemarkie. The sea shore is best about an hour after high tide; when the tide is low, waders, ducks and geese are too far out to be seen easily.

Central Highlands

You do not have to go very far north to see many of the highland birds. In Perthshire there are beautiful glens, mountains and lochs. The near perfect cone of Schiehallion holds ptarmigan, and to the south of Loch Earn, Ben Vorlich offers a wonderful climb. Look out for peregrine on Ben Lawers which also has an interesting flora, and there are some well-trodden peaks to the north of it. The lonelier hills will be frequented by eagles.

Between Bridge of Balgie and Loch Lyon blackcock may be seen at their leks beside the road. Go and find your own remote hill loch above Glen Turret, Glen Almond or Glen Lyon or in the hills north of Aberfeldy. Peregrine, dunlin, ring ouzel - in rocky places, - grouse, curlew, common sandpiper, snipe, golden plover, and dipper may all be found. Many of these will also be met with along the rivers, where goosander and merganser breed. And over at the Loch of Lowes near Dunkeld you can get excellent views of the osprey and many other exciting species. (See East Coast Section). Among breeding birds in the woods of Perthshire are redstart, spotted flycatcher, wood and willow warblers, buzzard, sparrow hawk, redpoll and great-spotted woodpecker.

Most ospreys spend the winter south of the Sahara and so do many insect eaters that are common in Scotland: willow warbler, tree pipit, spotted flycatcher, redstart, whinchat, cuckoo, swallow, swift, house martin and sand martin. The longer hours of daylight in summer in northern climes give them more time for feeding their broods. The song of the willow warbler from woods or bushes all over Scotland is one of the sounds of early summer. On the moors it is replaced by the trill of the ubiquitous meadow pipit. Another bird noticeably common along hedge or wall or around rocks, even at considerable heights is the wren.

Along moorland roads the whinchat too is very frequently seen, often perched on telegraph wires. In Scotland the chaffinch often seems to replace the sparrow as a haunter of farmyards and back gardens - what an improvement!

In the Eastern Cairngorms Balmoral Forest is a good place for capercaillie and there are lovely streams where the goosander is likely. There are some fine wild mountains in the Ben Avon group as well. And so, over the bleak grouse moors on the Tomintoul road, we come to Speyside and its wonderfully varied habitats. The osprey is here again at Loch Garten under the protection of the R. S. P. B. And in the old Caledonian pine forest of Abernethy are a host of other attractions.

The crested tit is the bird of Speyside though happily it can now be found in a number of other places in the highlands. It is a bird of the old Caledonian forest. Coal tits too prefer conifers and the caper is as likely in Abernethy forest as anywhere. Rothiemurchus to the west also has crested tits. The larch woods around Loch an Eilean are a haunt of crossbills and siskins. The birch woods of Craigellachie Nature Reserve near Aviemore are full of birds.

Buzzard

For easy viewing of ptarmigan the ski lift takes you almost to the top of Cairngorm. On the high flat tops throughout the Grampion range there is a chance of dotterel. This rare and very friendly little bird - perhaps there is an unhappy connection between the two characteristics - shares with the red-necked phalarope an interesting reversal of the sex roles. The female is dominant in courting behaviour and after she has laid the eggs the cock is left to brood them and to rear the chicks. To this end, he is less brightly coloured than the hen bird. The snow bunting can be found in the Cairngorms but it is very elusive. The great corries of Braeriach are worth exploring. There's a long and beautiful walk up Glen Einich and as it becomes wilder eagles are more likely. Glen Feshie and the valley of the Findhorn going up into the Monadliaths are also good eagle sites. In all these places the usual birds of river, moor and mountain may be found: merganser, greenshank, redshank, curlew, golden plover, buzzard, raven and many others.

On the fringes of the central highlands there are several lochs worth mentioning. Loch Ruthven and its companion loch over by Loch Ness should have Slavonian grebes breeding on them, while to the south the hill lochs above Loch Laggen are often good for divers. Finally there is Lochindorb North West of Grantown. A minor road runs along the loch and at the far end there is a lovely walk in deserted country. You may see golden plover, grouse, curlew, meadow pipits, kestrel, redshank, wigeon, oystercatcher and goosander.

For birdwatchers there's a wonderful spot to stay - a farm called Connage which lies about 3 miles out of Grantown on the A939. You see the lane to the farm on the right going towards Tomintoul, you really need a car. The field behind the farm has red grouse, curlew, oystercatcher, lapwing, and golden plover. Their calls and the bleating of sheep are the only sounds in an idyllic setting.

Argyll and Loch Lomand Area

Scotland is lucky in that there is superb bird watching to be had within easy reach of its great conurbations. A short drive north of Glasgow, the Loch Lomond National Nature Reserve lies in the South East corner of Loch Lomond. In winter large flocks of duck and geese are to be found there. You should contact the warden in Drymen. From Aberfoyle you can reach the Queen Elizabeth Forest Park. The views of Ben Lomond from Loch Ard are glorious and it is an excellent area for all predators except golden eagle. There are also large blackcock leks. Get in touch with the head forester in Aberfoyle.

At Tarbet on the west shore of Loch Lomond the road turns off to Arrochar. On the other side of Loch Long the Argyll National Forest Park covers 60,000 acres.

Here an assortment of relatively accessible peaks offer good viewing of mountain birds. The scenery too is magnificent with sea lochs cutting deep inland. Ben Narnain and Ben Vorlich (not the Loch Earn one) are most likely to have ptarmigan.

Those who continue northwards from Loch Lomond up the A82 should turn off at Bridge of Orchy for an ideal bird watching holiday - especially in spring and early summer when they can watch blackcock lekking and the greenshank's display flight. A road goes along Loch Tulla to the Black Mount estate. Among the trees you will find the Inveroran Hotel, and can exchange the noise of traffic for the music of a burn. Good paths meander around both sides of the loch and in the woods. Blackcock, greenshank, goldeneye, common sandpiper, goosander, and merganser can all be seen. A path leads westwards from the loch up to Loch Dochard. This is glorious. country. The magnificent bulk of Stob Chabhar towers on the right. There should be eagles in the corries behind it at the head of Loch Ba. We saw many deer, and grouse they jumped up, startled, among the heather. There were seven whooper swans on Loch Dochard. The intrepid with camping equipment can go on down Glen Kinglass to beautiful Loch Etive. But you can drive down Glen Etive to reach the loch. The road is not much frequented, perhaps because most people are pressing on for Glen Coe where history should take precedence over ornithology. But Glen Etive should not be missed for its beauty and variety of habitat. The high cols are a wonderful setting for eagle sightings and there are redstarts in the woods. As you cross Rannoch Moor keep an eye open for curlew, buzzard, whimbrel, and golden plover. The minor road to Glen Etive turns off to the left after you have passed Kingshouse Hotel and crossed the River Etive. Another expedition worth making is to take the White Corries ski-lift. You'll soon find ptarmigan on the high top and will have magnificent views of Stob Dearg. We found frogs at over 2,000 feet. When we were at Loch Tulla in summer we received great kindness and help from the Black Mount estate. The keeper told us where we could go to be out of the way of stalkers and we were made to feel very welcome.

From Loch Tulla one can reach Oban either down Glen Orchy and round the top of Loch Awe and the pass of Bran-

Fulmar, see page 25

Rooks, see page 7

Puffin, see page 27

Red Grouse, see page 8

The Bass Rock Gannets, see page 5

Kittiwakes, see page 12

"*Conversation*" *with Turnstone, see page 24*

Razor Bills, see page 11

Eider Drake, see page 11

der, or via Ballachulish and down Loch Linnhe and Loch Creran where you are nearly always on the shores of a sea loch. Oban is the port for a visit to Mull (of which more later) and in winter it is one of the best places to see great northern divers. Even in summer there are often non-breeding birds about. The west coast of Argyll south of Oban is not well known and one can spend a quiet bird watching holiday amid beautiful scenery. Kilmelford is well placed for expeditions into the hills or along the coast and the Cuilfail Hotel will feed you well after a day in the open air. A glance at the ordnance survey map shows innumerable lochans scattered everywhere. It's just a matter of finding one with your own pair of red-throated or black-throated divers. Look out for eagles too. We saw black-throats on the largish loch by the road between Kilmelford and Loch Avich and found red-throats on Kilchoan Loch and its partner up in the hills from a track that goes out to Degnish point. This track turns off along the head of Loch Melfort. Come down for half an hour in the evening and sit in the car by the marshy fringes of the loch. You may see a heron fishing or the hen harrier hunting very close to you over the fields. The male is a graceful bird, a lovely pale grey with white rump and long tail. The track to Degnish soon ceases to be tarred but, although not good in places, is perfectly negotiable by a normal car with a competent driver. Degnish is a farm, it must have one of the loveliest situations in Scotland. A path goes past the farm and down to the point. You can spend a day there with terns and herons fishing all around, kestrels and buzzards overhead, twites twittering among the rocks, and an otter to share the beach with you. From Kilmelford it's worth visiting Lochs Scamadale and Tralaig, and Inverinan Forest and Loch Avich are interesting and beautiful too.

Further south Kintyre is almost unexplored as a holiday centre because it is rather far along the road to nowhere. The eagle and the hen harrier can be found and most of the highland and coastal birds. In winter large numbers of great northern diver, eider, long-tailed duck, slavonian grebe, and velvet scoter can be seen on West Loch Tarbet.

Off the coast lies Islay (prounced 'Ila') beckoning all bird watchers. Perhaps my special feeling of affection for Islay has something to do with the weather. Out of seven days spent there, six and a half had unbroken sunshine! Bowmore is a good centre at which to stay, and a pleasant little township with its harbour and round church. The peculiar shape of Islay makes it important to be centrally situated. On the Mull of Oa in the extreme south is probably the only breeding colony of choughs in Scotland. You can watch them at close quarters, and enjoy fine cliff scenery too. Auks nest on the cliffs here and elsewhere and terns on the beaches. In the south east are woods holding woodcock, sparrowhawk, and fallow deer, while along the coast are some charming little bays. Claggain Bay is the largest but just to the north the shore is delightfully isolated at Ardtalla.

The great birding areas are in the northern half of the island. On the flats around the head of Loch Indaal, godwits, curlew and a host of other waders will be feeding. Ardnave is a wonderful area. Drive up the west side of Loch Gruinart and walk along a path going north round the left hand side of Ardnave House. Follow it to the sea. Sunsets here are very fine and you may see mergansers, godwits, and curlew. If you take the road further to the west instead of going up Loch Gruinart you will end up at Sanaigmore, and can walk out to the bay. On the cliffs there are fulmars and rock doves, with gannets often visible at sea. As you drive back, make a detour round Loch Gorm to visit the Atlantic strands of Saligo Bay, and Machir Bay, with mergansers, fulmars, shags and gannets off shore. On the Rhinns look out for the hen harrier and inland too you may see blackcock or the corncrake. Eagle eyries are on some sea cliffs. At Port Askaig gannets and shearwaters can often be seen passing through the sound of Islay, and the black guillemot nests. Go north from here to Bonhaven and then walk out to the North East point. There are some fine raised beaches in this isolated area.

The boat to Islay also serves Colonsay which reproduces in miniature all the island habitats except high peaks, with the addition of rich woodlands and gardens to shelter small birds. There are cliffs with sea bird colonies and sand dunes with nesting terns.

If Islay is idyllic in summer with its 100 species of breeding birds, it is an ornithologist's dream in winter. By February there are some 10,000 barnacle geese - one sixth of the world population. They breed in Greenland, arriving on Islay late in October and remaining until April. They are handsome, black and white geese and the sound of their 'conversation' and the noise of their wings when thousands take to the air is unforgettable. Loch Indaal and Loch Gruinart hold the greatest concentrations. Many white-fronts and greylag winter on Islay too, and everywhere there are masses of waders and duck - golden plover, dunlin, curlew, godwits, purple sandpiper, scaup, eider, goldeneye, wigeon, tufted. And in mid-winter you have the island almost to yourself - and the birds! It is perhaps easier then to go by air - it only takes an hour and a half from Glasgow and you have wonderful views of the Arran mountains. You can hire a car on Islay.

The other large Hebridean island that is part of Argyll is Mull. If I had to recommend only one of the Hebrides for a visit I should find it difficult to choose between Mull and Lewis - Harris which to the tourist counts as one island. Ornithologically the choice should go to Islay, but the other two have the advantage of grander mountains. The boat sails from Oban to Craignure. The Salen Hotel makes a good centre. The dining room has a lovely view, and swallows and house martins nest around the hotel. Habitats are varied on Mull and everywhere the great sea lochs add to the beauty of the scene. The road south from Craignure runs through sheltered woods, and after Lochdonhead a minor road turns off to Grass Point, a good place for turnstone and ringed plover and passing sea birds. Further on another road turns off for Loch Buie where many herons are likely to be seen.

The road from Salen across to Loch na Keal frequently has buzzards perched on the telegraph posts. Many people will tell you that they have seen an eagle on a telegraph post - eagles do not perch on telegraph posts! But you will often see eagles, and buzzards, sea birds, and ravens too, along the menacing cliffs of the Gribun. You won't know which way to look - inland to the cliffs or out to sea for the birds on Loch na Keal. At times great rafts of manx shearwaters pass up the loch. The road climbs steeply up behind the Gribun. You should allow half an hour on the homeward journey so that you can stop on the bend above Balmeanach farm and enjoy the perfection of the view - the massive cliffs of the Wilderness towering above the tiny, vividly green fields around the farm and the island-strewn loch stretching away to the distant Treshnish Isles.

These islands are well worth a visit. They are of basalt like Staffa. Thousands of sea birds nest there including kittiwakes, puffins, fulmars, guillemots, shags, cormorants, manx shearwaters and storm petrels. The storm petrel 'dances' on the surface of the water using its feet as it feeds on plankton. Thus it acquired its name - after the apostle Peter. It does not nest on the mainland anywhere in Britain, but only on small islands. A launch goes out to the Treshnish Isles from Ulva Ferry on certain days in the week. It is necessary to book in advance. On the way to Ulva Ferry along the north shore of Loch Indaal you will have magnificent views of Ben More, and beyond on Loch Tuath, divers are frequently seen feeding. In the north west of the island a road goes off for Croig. The old harbour was used by the drovers coming from the outer isles and taking their cattle across Mull and over to the mainland at Grass Point. The rocky headland and sandy bays beyond have superb views beyond Ardnamurchan Point to Rhum, Eigg and Skye. Divers, guillemots and other seabirds may be seen passing the point.

If you want to visit a really solitary and isolated area take a track along the north shore of Loch Scridain to the headland of Burg and walk northwards over to the Wilderness. At one point as we looked back down the valley below us we found we were looking at a golden eagle quartering the moor. It's not often you can look down on an eagle! Later we surprised a herd of eleven stag at a wallow, one of them a twelve pointer. It was an area of enormous scattered boulders like miniature mountains. Altogether we saw over a hundred deer and snipe, curlew, buzzard and kestrels. Another good walk is up Loch Ba and Glen Connel. Loch Ba has a sand martin colony and you may see divers, eagles, herons, ravens, buzzards, hen harriers, kestrels and curlew.

Down in the south west the Ross of Mull and Iona present a quite different scene. This an area of soft springy turf, flowers and sand dunes. Wrens and wheatears abound on Iona. The curlew and oystercatcher call along the beaches. Gannets dive in the sound of Iona. Tranquility is the keynote in this sunlit landscape, a tranquility emphasised by the simple lines of the cathedral on a site that has been a place of pilgrimage and faith through so many centuries.

From Oban and possibly from Tobermory, boats go to Coll and Tiree and you can fly to Tiree. Coll is rocky and peaty. The red-throated diver and the arctic skua nest there, and also on Tiree. Tiree's Gaelic name means the kingdom beneath the waves and Tiree is very nearly just that! Most of it is only a few feet above sea level. The Atlantic winds and waves have broken down the soil to a fine sand and it is, like parts of the Outer Hebrides, an island of fertile white sand. But there are also cliffs for breeding sea birds. Tufted duck and shelduck breed and there are large colonies of terns especially on the islet of Gunna between Coll and Tiree.

Oyster Catcher

North-West

The North West - for a fortunate few that phrase will always mean Scotland - the real Scotland - north of the Great Glen. And more especially it means the coast, that magical land of loch and mountain and forest where, even when you look away from the sea, there seems to be more water than land. But before he heads for the great fiords of the coast, the birdwatcher will be wise to search out an inland glen, Glen Affric. It claims to be the most beautiful of Scottish glens and I would not dispute the claim. Go south from Inverness or north from Fort Augustus along the west side of Loch Ness until you reach Drumnadrochit.

Glen Urquhart leads you along a broad fertile valley towards Glen Affric. But there's much to see on the way. Turn off to the right up Glen Convinth, though the A833 doesn't seem much like an A road. After a few miles you come to a loch on the left. You can pull off on the knoll above it and view from the car or scramble through the bog to sit among the heather on the other side. This tiny lochan holds a wealth of bird life, including a pair of Slavonian grebe. They are quite tame birds and their 'weed dance' is fascinating. It is preceded by a high rippling trill and both birds bow and stretch their necks several times, and then, with weed trailing from their beaks, they appear to scamper side by side along the surface of the water, in fact almost out of it. In breeding plumage they are lovely creatures with bright russet necks and golden ear tufts or 'horns' from which they get their other name of horned grebe. This little lochan is a real 'find'. Besides the grebes there's a noisy colony of common gulls and many other things turn up - wigeon, teal, goldeneye, - while curlew, snipe and redshank call and feed around its shores. One single-minded redshank kept returning to a pool - no more than a puddle - not two yards from our car. Whenever a car passed on the road behind, it would fly away at the last minute in fool-hardy fashion across the road. I fear its days were numbered. The Slavonian grebe builds a floating platform for a nest and is a very rare bird in Britain. Loch Laide, along minor roads to the east, has about half a dozen pairs, but its situation is less attractive. You can actually see a house or two!

Back in Glen Urquhart there's a heronry just south of the road. You can watch it easily from the roadside. While we were there a tractor was ploughing an awkward corner below three nests. At first all the birds got off, but one returned. For nearly an hour the other two birds flew around or perched at some distance, mobbed by rooks. Were these two inexperienced or timid birds, or was it because the other nest was very slightly further from the tractor? It seemed touch and go whether the herons would return before two hoodies braved the one heron still on its nest. The fields were crowded with rooks and at Polmailly House Hotel there's a large rookery. The house and grounds are set back from the road at the foot of attractive hills. An ideal place for a birdwatcher to stay in spring!

Glen Affric in spring is perfect. First you drive through woods to Dog Falls where there's a remnant of the old Caledonian forest on the other side of the river. A walk up there may discover capers. crossbills and siskins. On Loch Beneveian red-throated divers and great crested grebes may be feeding. At Affric Lodge a path leads to the right of the house along Loch Affric. Starting off quietly, you may get close to greenshank on the marshy bit by the house. On the shores of the loch just here oyster-catcher, curlew, and redshank call and feed. Wheatears are everywhere, and the meadow pipit planes up and down in display flight. You can walk five miles along the loch. The beauty is breathtaking and eagles are quite likely to soar over at any minute. Look in the pine trees for crested tits and siskins. At the far end there's another green marshy flat with duck and waders - greenshank again, wigeon and teal. The path goes on over the hills for many, many miles to Kintail.

From Cannich the main road goes up Strathglass. The minor road on the other side of the river is even more attractive. In spring whooper swans may be lingering and in the birchwoods roe deer are often seen. At Struy Bridge you turn off for Glen Strathfarrar. You must obtain a permit in the village to have the gate unlocked for you. This is a superb glen for birdwatching. There's a black-cock lek in an open area in the woods right by the road. It's a good area for roe deer too. The glen is dotted with marshy patches and riverside flats frequented by duck and waders. At the west end of a loch there's a small knoll where you can spend a day watching peregrine, raven and buzzard all feeding young on the cliffs that run back along-side the loch. There's an eagle eyrie too, but it's not always occupied. Below there will probably be whoopers, mergansers, goldeneye, and red-throats on the loch.

The road to the isles is also the road to Arisaig and Mallaig. Every little bay on the Rhu peninsular at Arisaig will have its waders and on Ardnish you may surprise a merlin. There's a wonderful walk over the hills from Loch Moror to Loch Nevis passing lochs with black-throated divers. Look out for eagles and red deer on the hills, and roe in the woods round Arisaig. From Mallaig boats make expeditions to Loch Scavaig on Skye and to Rhum and Eigg. On the journey you'll have good views of shearwaters, guillemots, gannets and other sea birds.

Rhum is controlled by the Nature Conservancy and used for research into deer management. Access is limited. Near the top of Askival at a height of 2,500 feet there is an interesting colony of several thousand pairs of manx shear-waters. They nest in burrows or holes. The manx shearwater is a fascinating bird. It spends all day at sea and only comes to its burrow after dark to avoid predatory gulls, because it is slow and clumsy on land, unable to walk properly. At sea it is a superb flier and a flight of them skimming the waves with a quick flash of silver is wonderful sight. During incubation one bird remains on the nest for long periods and the changeover after dark is accompanied by weird and unearthly calls. In a large colony it's an experience not likely to be forgotten. The shearwaters from Skokholm off the Welsh coast go all the way to the Bay of Biscay to feed on sardines but no one has certainly proved where the Scottish birds go to feed.

There is a car ferry to Skye from Mallaig but no road up the west coast. The coastal road north starts at Loch Duich and for that you must start back in the Great Glen and go via Loch Garry and Glen Shiel. The Five Sisters of Kintail provide some of the most spectacular scenery in Scotland and one need not now forgo them for fear of endless delays at Strome Ferry. A new road round Loch Carron by-passes all that. Soon after Kishorn the road to Applecross turns off - the only Alpine road in Britain! You may see eagles in a setting truly worthy of them.

After that detour a grand road goes to Shieldaig and round Loch Torridon. There's a minor road along the northern shore that could be the starting point of many a memorable walk. And there's the stupendous ridge walk of Liathach for the skilled and courageous. Another expedition that only requires stamina is up to Coire Mhic Fhearchair in the heart of Ben Eighe. This is eagle, peregrine and ptarmigan country, the haunt of deer and wild cat. It's National Nature Reserve and contains a remnant of Caledonian pine forest - siskin, redstart, woodcock, goldcrest, crossbill, and long-eared owl may all be found. On the other side of Loch Maree, Slioch awaits the mountain walker. Kinlochewe is a good centre from which to enjoy all this.

The road meanders on through Gairloch and round Loch Broom. It takes half a day up here to cover fifty miles as the crow flies, but you must not miss a minute of it. About 10 miles north of Ullapool a minor road turns off for Loch Inver. If you follow it to the sea and beautiful Achnahaird Bay you will come round to Achiltibuie opposite the Summer Isles. This is a place to linger for a few days. There will be waders at Achnahaird Bay if you can take your eyes from the view, especially at sunset. Stac Polly is the popular climb but Ben More Coigach is grander and likely to hold ptarmigan. You can get a boat to the Summer Isles which are well known bird haunts.

As you travel on through Lochinver and up to Clashnessie the landscape has a dream-like quality. Water, water everywhere and the strange shapes of Suilven, Canisp and Quinag only exceeding in size a hundred others equally fantastic. It is superb diver country. Loch Drumbeg often has a pair. There are merlin too and on the Stoer peninsular you may surprise a peregrine at its kill and get quite close, so unused is the bird to disturbance. From the cliffs at Clashnessie watch out for gannets, guillemots, fulmars, kittiwakes and terns.

Across the Kylesku Ferry and on to the north lies Badcall Bay. Does Caladh still do bed and breakfast? The view defies description. Take a rowing boat out and potter among the islands. Get up early and find a loch a little way up into the hills where the divers will be shattering the quiet with their wild haunting cries. Perhaps an eagle will be circling over to the east where the graceful peak of Ben Stack soars skywards. Red-throated divers are usually found on small lochs. They nest there and usually feed at sea - though not those in Glen Affric. Black-throats nest on large lochs and feed on the loch where they nest.

Between Scourie and Laxford Bridge a road turns off for Handa. A boat will take you across from Tarbet. The seabird colonies on the cliffs are fantastic. Peregrine, skua and diver have all nested too. Down this road you can also get to Fanagmore and sit high above Loch Laxford watching the seals. There are black-throats on Loch Stack. For a walk that can scarcely be equalled take the path near Lochstack Lodge going towards Arkle. At first you are beside a lush flower-edged stream, but soon out on the moor where the path skirts a couple of lochs and winds round below the bare slopes of Arkle. There are almost sure to be deer and eagles up here. You are heading for Loch an Easain Uaine or the Loch of the Green Falls in the great horseshoe where Arkle curves round to meet Foinaven. At the far end of the loch snow buntings are said to nest.

Going north again - and a glance at the ordnance survey

map shows that the peninsular southwest of Loch Inchard might well repay investigation. There are probably many diver lochs and many bays as beautiful as Badcall and Clashnessie. That's the glory of Ross and Sutherland - anywhere you can find your own private loch or bay or headland and it feels as if no one has ever set foot there before.

At Durness you have reached the north coast after a memorable journey. But with the sands of Balnakiel Bay and the flowery meadows between little Loch Lunlish (where you might see Slavonian grebe) and the cliffs it doesn't seem very northerly. At Faraid Head there are excellent sea bird cliffs and stacks. If you can overcome the problems of getting across to the great unexplored slab that ends in Cape Wrath, the cliffs of Clo Mor, nearly sheer at over 800 feet, are the highest on the mainland of Britain. Clo Mor is famous for its seabird colonies, the ptarmigan breeds in this area at a much lower level than normal and there's a constant stream of gannets passing off shore.

At Durness the Cave of Smoo is worth a visit, and as you go down the cliff path you may notice a large grey ball of downy fluff on a ledge. It's a young fulmar. Beware the line of fire! The fulmar's defence is to emit a stream of evil smelling oil for a surprising distance and with great accuracy! It is fitting that a sea bird should have the last word in such a land of water. The road goes on magnificently round Loch Eriboll and the Kyle of Tongue. Ben Hope and Ben Loyal are glorious mountains too before you head south for the modern world again.

Skye, Outer Hebrides, Orkney's and Shetland's

Skye is a slight disappointment to the ornithologist. After Islay, Mull and the lovely wildernesses of Sutherland it seems rather overpopulated. But the north is beautiful and good for eagles. On Vatternish near Ardmor you will perhaps see otters playing on the shore or a stoat running along a wall. Perhaps, as you sit on cliffs 1,000 feet high at Dunvegan Head, a pair of eagles will swoop past you out of the mist not ten yards away. The Quirang is an amazing place.

From Uig on Skye the car ferries leave for the Elysian

isles of the Outer Hebrides. Here the golden eagle nests and hunts at much lower altitudes than on the mainland. The islands are very good for eagles especially in late summer months. The ferry takes you to Loch Maddy on North Uist. From the top of Beinn Moor or Beinn Bhreac you will have wonderful views and may well see eagles, buzzards, ravens, hen harriers, golden plover and snipe. Griminish Point at the North West tip of North is a good place for seeing shearwaters, gannets, fulmars, peregrine and curlew. At Balranald on the west coast the R. S. P. B. have a reserve where many birds breed - gadwall, wigeon, shoveler, water rail, merganser, terns, corncrake, and sometimes the red-necked phalarope.

On South Uist, Loch Druidibeg is a National Nature Reserve and the principal British nesting ground of the greylag goose. Permission to visit in the breeding season should be obtained in advance from the warden at Loch-boisdale. Loch Bee has a vast colony of breeding mute swans and usually a few whoopers in summer. Of course in winter there will be masses of geese and whoopers in the Hebrides. The arctic skua nests in South Uist. Loch Eynort is a wonderful area. Take your car as far as possible along the northern side and then ramble round its shores and out to the sea. You may see ravens, buzzards, herons, peregrine, kestrel, redshank, knot, greenshank, curlew, divers, shearwaters and gannets. Herons nest on an island in the loch. At Lochboisdale they nest on the cliffs and in North Uist there are some ground nesting herons in the Loch Scadavay region.

In contrast to the craggy lochs, the peat moors and mountains of the east side of the Outer Hebrides, the west coast has been pounded by the Atlantic into long, smooth bays of white shell sand. The land has also been manured with seaweed and there are arable farms, and the springy turf and beautiful flowering meadows of the machair. Here there are tern colonies, waders feeding along the shore and the hen harrier hunting over the fields. Rubha Ardvule is a good place, but you can choose your own lonely strand. The corncrake used to be widespread throughout Britain - now it is holding on as a breeding bird in North West Scotland and the island where the hay is still made and carried in traditional fashion. Mechanisation and the early cutting for silage has meant death to the corncrake broods.

At the southern-most tip of the Outer Hebrides are the islands of Berneray and Mingulay. Their cliffs are famous and breeding seabirds are numbered in thousands of pairs. Berneray has around 10,000 pairs each of kittiwakes, guillemots and razorbills. Trips are made to the islands from Barra which is reached by car ferry from Lochbois-dale (or Oban). There is also a car ferry to Lochboisdale from Mallaig and a new one to Stornaway in Lewis from Ullapool. There's an airport at Stornaway.

Lewis and Harris is a large island and so cut up by sea lochs that road distances are great. The Uig-Valtos area in the North East corner is one of the best - merlin, pere-grine, eagle, greenshank and black-throated diver all breed in the area. You may have the astonishing luck to meet a merlin plucking a small wader in the middle of the road, and in no hurry at all to depart! On the shell sand beaches or their marshy edges there are knot, dunlin, and golden plover. Uig Bay is lovely, so is Traig na Beiridhe where the sand has a pink tinge and exquisite pink, lilac and yellow shells may be collected. The point at Crothair on Gt. Bernera is a good place to see terns. But there are thousands of bays and headlands to choose from - all beautiful, all deserted, all rich in bird life. On your way to the Butt of Lewis the standing stones of Callanish des-serve a visit. If you are at the magnificent cliffs around the Butt of Lewis after rough weather tremendous seas will be breaking on the rocks. Gannets and fulmars are continually passing on their way to Sula Sgeir and St. Kilda. At Port of Ness you can watch manx shearwaters passing up and down, and maybe sooty shearwaters. The loch nearby is good for many birds too.

The lochs and mountains and islands of Lewis and Har-ris are comparatively unexplored and there are opportunit-ies for the adventurous to find new breeding species. Does Leach's petrel nest on an island in Loch Roag?

The high hills of Harris are typical eagle country but on the islands you often find eagles in unexpected places. On Toe Head we had frequent and close views of eagles. Toe Head has magnificent views across a wide sandy bay and back to Renish Point, south across the Sound of Harris and to the mountains of North Harris. Another wonderful spot is Husinish Bay and Point, or round the coast from Husinish to Loch Resort. You will leave the western isles most unwillingly - they are unsurpassed birding areas.

There are many outlying islands that are bird haunts but difficult to reach, the Flannan Isles and North Rona for instance. But none are more famed in literature and the hearts of ornithologists than St. Kilda. It lies in the Atlantic 45 miles west of North Uist - a tiny group of islands with the highest sheer cliffs in the British Isles. St. Kilda's population, which had dwindled to 36, left it in 1930. It is now a National Nature Reserve and is used as a radar tracking station. One is allowed to visit it but a visit is difficult to arrange. The National Trust for Scotland may still include it in its Islands Cruises. 40,000 pairs of gannets nest on St. Kilda - the largest gannetry in the world - and very similar numbers of fulmars. But these are outnumbered by puffins of which there are close on half a million. The rare Leach's petrel breeds there and St. Kilda has its own wren. The inhabitants relied largely on gannets and other sea birds for their food. Perilous expeditions were made to the stacks to collect young gannets. Fulmar fowling on the cliffs of the main island of Hirta began on August 12th. The young fulmars had to be quickly killed and their necks given a special twist to prevent the valuable oil escaping. This oil was the St. Kildan's source of light in the long dark winter. 'The Life and Death of St. Kilda' by Tom Steel is a most interesting account of a unique community.

North of John O'Groats are the Orkneys, reached by sea from Aberdeen, or by air. They are generally rather low though there are many sea bird cliffs especially on Hoy (where there is a hostel: inquiries to Youth Leader, Education Office, Kitkwall). The hen harrier breeds on the Orkneys which earlier in this century was its last refuge in Britain, but it has fortunately returned to some other parts of Scotland. Artic and great skuas breed and on Lochs Stenness and Harray the nesting population includes tern, eider, merganser, tufted duck, and dunlin. While in this area you should visit Scara Brae which has a wonderful coastal situation.

The Shetland Isles are only 6° south of the Arctic Circle. They have a culture and quality all their own. Access is by boat from Aberdeen to Lerwick or by air to Sumburgh. The list of breeding birds makes exciting reading. Peregrine on Fitful Head, storm petrel on Fetlar and Yell, manx shearwater on Fetlar, skuas, merlin, golden plover, merganser, eider, corncrake, red-necked phalarope, wigeon and pintail - and the usual seabirds on the magnificent cliffs everywhere and especially at Noss, Ronas Hill, Fitful Head, and Hermaness. The snowy owl and the whimbrel breed nowhere else in Britain. In winter and spring it is a good place for long-tailed duck. And with it all, the scenery is quite 'out of this world'.

For a really unusual holiday take the 'Good Shepherd' to Fair Isle where you can stay at the bird observatory. If bird observatories conjure up visions of sleeping bags and peeling potatoes and dormitory accommodation you'll probably find things rather different. Certainly in the days of Kenneth Williamson's wardenship there were hot water bottles in the beds, a roaring fire in the lounge at 8.30 a.m., and it was worth going all that way to sample his wife's cooking! Fair Isle has a crofting community, impressive cliffs, vast crowds of gossiping fulmars - 'marlies on the banks' as the Fair Islanders say onomatopoeically - and a reputation for rarities. Anything may turn up on migration in spring and autumn, short-toed lark, black-eared wheatear, subalpine warbler, citrine wagtail, steppe grey shrike, scarlet grosbeak. It's a great place for tickers'. But if you hover around the traps all day you will miss the essence of Fair Isle: the sheer goes where the sea runs in and the sea birds wheel and cry - some of them only specks on the water below, - the friendly village in the south, the sunlit cliffs along the east side by Sheep Craig.

Useful Addresses

Nature Conservancy (for National Nature Reserves).
12, Hope Terrace,
Edinburgh 9.

National Trust for Scotland (organizes occasional working parties to St. Kilda)
Secretary,
5, Charlotte Square,
Edinburgh 2.

Forestry Commission (list of publications and leaflet on camping):

25, Drumsheugh Gardens,
Edinburgh 3.

R.S.P.B.:

21, Regent Terrace,
Edinburgh 7.

Scottish Tourist Board:

2, Rutland Place,
Edinburgh 1.

Bird Observatories:

Isle of May, Firth of Forth.   Free prospectus:

Alastair MacDonald,
Hadley Court,
Haddington,
E. Lothian.

Fair Isle.   Free prospectus:

Hon. Sec Fair Isle Bird Observatory Trust,
21, Regent Terrace,
Edinburgh 7.
or: The Warden (1st. April - 30th. November).
Fair Isle. (Tel: Fair Isle 8).

Books to Read

F. Fraser Darling: Natural History in the Highlands and Islands.
Seton Gordon: A Highland Year (or any other works).
Tom Steel: The Life and Death of St. Kilda.
K. Williamson and J. Morton Boyd: A Mozaic of Islands.

Index